Sept. 25, 1997

To Rob Carlisle,

whose passion for Cape Cod is matched by his Renaissance gifts,

with admiration,

Christopher Bonanos

Pilgrim at Sunset

Martin C. Rosner, M.D.

Triangle Books

For my wife, Arlene,
who has always been with me in search of the poetry in life,
and for my childen, who are my enduring happiness.

Triangle Books
are published by
Research Triangle Publishing, Inc.
PO Box 1223
Fuquay-Varina, NC 27526

Copyright © 1994 by Martin C. Rosner, MD
All rights reserved. This book, or parts thereof,
may not be reproduced in any form without permission.

ISBN 1-884570-04-6

Cover Design by Art House

Printed in the United States of America
10 9 8 7 6 5 4 3 2 1

Contents

Testament	1
Something Awful	2
Incantation	3
The Veil of Maya	4
Soliloquy, Sleepless Night	5
Ballad (with thanks to Robbie Burns)	6
On the Question of Femininity	7
Beauty, Flesh and Blood	8
Still Life	9
Karma	10
Reflections, Deflections	11
Fire Nights	12
At The Burning Ghats, Nepal	13
Midnights	14
Easter in Ireland	15
Wind Solo	16
When the Bugle Sounds Recall	17
Pilgrim at Sunset	18
Morning on the Marsh	19
On the Tidal Flats	20
The Neighbors	21
Saltmarsh	22
The Garden by the Sea	23
Longwood	24
The Doctor in the Garden	25
Sons and Dreams	26
At The Turning of the Glass	27
City Courtyard	28
Echoes: 1949	29
Beyond the Maze	30
Galileo	31
Epitaph	31

Testament

In the outback stretches of the night
As I unroll the maps that mark my route
From then to now,
It comes:
Like some silent, savage beast that stalks
And waits, it crouches , shapeless, in the room
And breathes in tempo with my pulse.
I cannot know if it will spring
Or merely contemplate its certain prey.
But it will come, the light-destroying leap,
And scatter maps like scraps
On windblown, vacant wastes.
If one flutters, ragged, at your feet,
Pick it up and read:
The legend and the dedication
Are for you.

Something Awful

Unless you choose to test your strength
Do not read on; this is a spell.
These words are glyphs of power
That slip unwanted into memory
As if inserted by a surgeon's hand,
To seal themselves away
In hippocampal dark, and linger.
Like a melody that haunts and taunts
To surface unrequested, unannounced,
Even when unwelcome, they will persist
And reemerge, redundant, independent
Of your will, unforgotten over years,
Waiting to assert their immortality,
To claim a portion of your life
Despite your opposition, to mock
Your feeble claim to rule your mind,
As I have just most cruelly done.

Incantation

Magic must be nurtured
Magic must be fed
Magic must be shielded
From artifice and dread.
Magic must have mystery
Melody and light
Just enough of verity
To keep illusion bright.
Gentleness born of sorrow
Gentleness born of grief
Gently gild the morrow
With magical belief.

The Veil of Maya

Sea-smells and honeysuckle mingle
Like the scent
Of Chinese cooking, mixing
Yearning and fulfillment
In a tidal flow.
Hunger is like that,
And so is love,
And all the mysteries that shelter
In the limbic cave.
To speak of synapses, of arcane
Chemicals that bridge those microgaps,
Is not the truth I seek,
No more than mind and brain
Explain the pain or joy
Or both that form my soul.
Like music is to notes,
Or vision is to sight,
To know the difference
Is to know.

Soliloquy, Sleepless Night

It's the black rose that I fear
You should have let it lie
Abandoned
Where I left it
Frozen
Safely in some mythic sleep
Interred
With pain and fear and loss
You should have let it lie
Within
That glacial place
That sealed
Away the stalking hunger
And the rage
I told you
It's the black rose that I fear
Yet you seized it
In your warm, unknowing hand
And let its perfume free
To mingle
With your skin
I hope your innocence
Learns power
That my experience
Knows grace
And that our sorcery
Together
Draws on faith

Ballad (with thanks to Robbie Burns)

Look back, look back, my laurel love,
Look back at the years gone by;
Look back over your shoulder, love,
For one sweet look and a sigh.

Look back, my lissome lady dear
To the lyric lass you were;
Look with burnished glance and mind
At you who grew from her.

And recollect her lute-song laugh
And the dance that marked her way;
And think how joyous she would be
To know she'd be you today.

On the Question of Femininity

I'd like to ask her why she shines
Like early summer sun
On a quiet pond in Maine;
But sorcerers can't spoil
Their spells, or spin them
Willy-nilly as they must.
I'd like to ask her why she flutes
When others bray;
But then she'd stop to think,
And then the music would stop, too,
And maybe lose its lustre
Or its joy.
If I ask her why she walks
The way a flower sways
In gentle air,
She'll be self-conscious
And sit down.
But anyway, I know the mix
Is partly artifice, and partly
Natural grace, and part response
To those very questions
That I raise.

Beauty, Flesh and Blood

Like a gazelle pursued by lions
On the green and deadly plain,
Her leaps were antigravitational,
And turns at speed bewildered
Cruelly clutching claws.
But nature has no amnesty
For beauty, and lions
Represent the writ of God.
Her grace remains a memory;
The rest sustains
The chain of life.

Still Life

Watching the sea from a balcony
I think of you as an odalisque
Lying on your side in a shadowed room
High above a tiny harbor
With the tide at the evening ebb.
You are caught by my mind, immobile,
Like a still life, with a table
Holding flowers that paint colors,
Faded reds and pallid gold,
On faintly glowing air that holds
The last dim aqueous light.
A wine bottle, nearly spent,
Stands neglected by the vase.
All seems nearly spent, drained,
The flowers, wine, the light,
The turning tide, the sounds
In the town below.
Yet you seem to hold it all
Together, refusing the curtain's fall.
I will not search for meaning
In this scene; I will not probe
And disarray the implications
Suspended in this frame.
So the incompleteness is on-going
And your mystery preserved;
And mine the magic
To lock it forever
Out of time.

Karma

Caparisoned for battle, he strode
Across the cosmic plain, hauled
His shield up hillsides, and lifted
High his sword at fords.
But stumbling on a fold in time
He found himself, anachronistic,
On a small suburban street.
He bartered armor for a suit
Of cloth alchemical, changed
His shield for motley plastic runes,
And his sword for magic metal
Flashing fiery ciphers at his touch,
Sheathed within the pocket of his coat.
But when sleep turned folds in time
To lattices to climb between the worlds,
His armor chafed his modern skin,
The shield-ache trembled in his arm,
And the sword-hilt twisted in his fingers,
As before.

Reflections, Deflections

Lewis Carroll loved the looking-glass
And so did Jean Cocteau.
Both knew a mirror is a doorway
Into paradox or truth
And sometimes both.
But Alice was a seer, sister to Cassandra,
Piping prophecies of mad inversions
In a world of total certainty
That collapsed in total doubt.
And Cocteau's poet, noble poet,
Stayed a poet,
Symbol without substance
Writer without writing
Thinker without thoughts
Voice without sound
Staring at a mirror
That would not let him pass.

Fire Nights

The fires of Beltane burn for the blood song,
And the fires of All Hallows heat the spirit dance;
But the bonfires of winter smoke silent
In the night, and sparks
Hemorrhage up to heaven
In a long, exhausted breath.
I only tend the fires,
I do not sing or dance.
But I watch through the seasons
As they spin their ordered course,
And I watch to see what watches
Where the fires' breath is lost.

At The Burning Ghats, Nepal

There is a river valley outside Katmandu
Where the burning ghats are never cool.
Tears and ashes mingle in the muddy stream
That undulates between its banks
Like a serpent, death clinging
To its coils.
Smoke spirals upward, black with grief,
Filters through the trees,
To linger outside dessicated caves
Where old and wizened men,
Milk-eyed and scabrous,
Sing reedy, baleful songs.
They laugh when taloned hands
Extend from rags to scuttle
On the stony floor, seizing
Blood and power
In some ancient, endless game.
Monkeys watch, alert and evil,
Like carved statues in a rite.
The bodies burn, the river runs,
The old men's games go on.
On the riverbank, around the ghats,
Stand Gurkha soldiers, just a few,
But men of legend, wearing valor
Like their skin.
Like me, I know
They are afraid.

Midnights

Sometimes a Roman candle
Lifts to rise and climb
To long orgasmic bursts
Across the black infinity
Of night.
But the moment of ignition
Burns perpetual
On the fuse that coils
From past to future
Through the midnights
Of my life.
It is my timeline
Arcing through the universe
From unseen origins
To unseen endings
Which begin again.
That radiance is scripted
For one agonizing instant
On the universial clock,
Just past the point
Of twelve, where
The timeline bends
To turn upon itself.

Easter in Ireland

The lambs are new in Kilkenny
This Good Friday, bright and green.
Collies plunge and dart, crowding
Calves to fresh pasture.
In the streets, mothers stroll sunward
With push-chairs, fat-fisted babies
Waving at the sky.
Fathers ease tight collars, proudly
Marshalling small scarecrows and Irish dolls
To church.
The bells and singing praise
The miracles, and call on all
To leave the sunlight
And the scent of fields and flowers
For the holy shadows
And the incense and the stone.
Spring turns its face to summer
With ancient, ineffable hope
That biology and spirit
Will magically combine.
It's locked within the chromosomes
This poignance, this passion,
This tropism for light,
Along with genes for heart attack
And cancer
And murder
And poetic second sight.

Wind Solo

The wind is ravening again.
My bed rocks under rushing clouds
And tilting skies, and the walls
Creak like canvas stretched
Against the wind.
No landmarks, no friendly stars,
My course a compromise
With nature and my will.
So be it.
Some use the charts,
Some make them,
Some journey where the weather
And the sea
Are all there is.

When the Bugle Sounds Recall

A time has come for stillness, to calm
The clamor of an urgent heart.
But what will grow in stillness?
Or does the noise and surge of life,
Much like a battle, recede to leave
The broken remnants on the field,
Sinking into rubble and decay?
Perhaps only weeds will grow,
And scavengers consume
What once was quick and bright,
Eager to contend?
No, one must ponder over stillness,
Walk the smoking, wounded ground;
Then inter the fallen, plow
And consecrate the field,
And wait to see
What grows.

Pilgrim at Sunset

Late, late afternoon
Of the day, of the year,
Of my light and my vision;
Here where the sun sets
On the outflung arm of America,
Cape Cod,
Still shaking its fist
And beckoning its fingers
At the world across the sea;
Here was the cutting edge of passion,
Half a millenium ago for those pilgrims
Who planted freedom on these shores,
Half a lifetime ago for me
Who found his own still growing here.
But the edge has turned
At the trailing edge of the century,
And thoughts that drove a nation
And a man
Seem almost elegaic, prized antiques
Within a modern house,
Dutifully displayed to guests
Somehow familiar
But impatient to move on.
Sunsets have such glory
That they still all nature's clamor
For a moment of sweet stillness
That passes through the afterglow
To the menace of the night;
And I watch and wait in silence
For the darkness that will come.
I know that empires pass,
That species die, that a man
Is just a spark of light
That kindles and is gone.
But this place still gives me courage
To believe in courage
And beginnings
And the dawn.

Morning on the Marsh

Alongside the marsh the road bends, turns
And clings, under pale, early sun.
Birds swoop and skim, darting
Over gently waving grasses, rising
High on trails of crystal sounds
That shimmer briefly in the lazy air.
Insects counterpoint in bass and tremolo,
Erratically, to lend a sense of expectation
Taking form within the quiet and the peace.
And then from somewhere back of time
A gentle, steady wind awakes.
It flows across the marsh in waves
Of rich, elusive smells
That verge on recollection
Of a life, a joy, an understanding
Not quite mine.

On the Tidal Flats

Alone between sea and dunes,
Under an enormous hemisphere of blue,
I wander through a land that opens
With the ebbing tide, to close again
When it returns with water fathoms deep.
I walk on sand flats tinged sporadically
The color of old blood, past
Tide pools incubating life, guarded
By gull sentries, and crabs concealed
In ambush, claws poised to demonstrate
The waiting, sudden savagery of life.
Though I may be only walking,
It is a pilgrimage in truth,
Into my past, and man's,
My senses searching for a knowledge
Left behind ten thousand years,
My mind attuned to messages
That language cannot grasp.
Countless times I have set out
Upon this pilgrimage, this hunt
For an elusive self
I hope is still preserved
Beneath the modern junk
That orbits in my brain.
So I listen for the coded message
Vibrating in the humming, onshore
Breeze, the sussurating voices
In the water rippling back,
And wait expectant for that moment
Of pure Zen, which will bring me
To my self, my many selves.

The Neighbors

A fox has come to be our neighbor, hunting
Rabbits in the near-by woods.
The rabbits eat our garden; the fox is welcome,
And he seems to know it, from the calm
He shows at meeting me at dusk
Upon a roadside trail; or even once
At night, when we dodged each other
As he stepped into my headlight beams
Upon the road.
It's plain he knows much more of man
Than I of fox. A backward glance
Or two to counterpoint his graceful trot
Is all I'm worth. He seems so sure
I won't return with horns and horses,
Dogs and death, to tear his brush
From rangy grace transformed
To bloody scraps.
He's right, you know. My childhood,
With its tales and all its wonder
Must be written on my face
Each time we meet.
So we are neighbors, if not friends

Saltmarsh

The marshes and the wetlands
Are disgorging to the sea;
Their rich and pungent odor
Wakes some sleeping life
In me, something ancient
Fierce and feral, open
Like the sea.
I breathe the wet, salt vapor
And some deep, old seal
Dissolves.
An essence stirs inside me
I do not know its name
It rushes past my reason
It surges out of me
For one incarnate instant
I know that I am free.

The Garden by the Sea

My garden is an oasis on the dune,
Buried in bayberry and beach plum
Dense enough to screen it
From the beach and from the road.
It crouches underneath the scathing winds
That come with sounds like shawms
Announcing devastating hordes,
And somehow draws in sun and rain
With steady doses of my anxious love,
And grows improbable, impractical and sweet.
To stumble on it suddenly, this tiny place
That nourishes the summer by a northern sea,
Is to encounter some ancient, arcane shrine
To a religion long-since gone.
It stirs some sleeping sense of awe
That prods and pushes at the modern mind,
As if your genes were shifting and retwining.
To meet the garden, unexpected,
Is to feel reworked and realigned,
Old and young at once,
Inexplicable, unfathomable, extending
From an unknown, yet familiar past
To richness yet to come.

Longwood

In Longwood gardens, joined
By genteel, goosey folk,
Live the pensioned plants,
Retired from their struggle
Towards the sun.
Like that former Duke
Of Bedford, who made
His grace a show,
They tolerate the viewers
Of their state.
Long since a wizard named Du Pont,
Who sired wizard progeny
Proved alchemist for this:
He turned black gunpowder
To gold, and gold
To plant and tree.

The Doctor in the Garden

Last harvest of summer, the garden
Stripped, except for a few forlorn
Flowers, like a middle-aged woman
Wearing earrings, in a doctor's
Examining gown.
In a sad, strange way
I am uplifted, tender.
I want to render dignity,
To speak in woodwind notes
Of what has been,
To celebrate the springtime scent
That lingers poignant
In a book within a drawer;
Commemorate the summer's
Reckless splendor fading
With her smile.
How can I comfort, with autumn
In my certain knowledge
And the truth that must be
Spoken with my words?
I tell her what I must,
Clear, gentle, and slow,
And that little flowers, little earrings,
Comfort us both.

Sons and Dreams

Last night I dreamed of my other son,
The one he used to be
Before he grew to be a man.
I still can hear the boyish voice,
The shiny liquid sounds an unexpected
Brook encountered in the wood.
My sleeping self is sure and clear,
But glad to put off scientific armor
And set aside the sword of doubt
To take the magic cup,
To play the self-indulgent, sentimental game.
I know he isn't there,
That he plays and scampers
Only in my dreams and recollections,
And in some few others
Who remember when.
And yet his presence is so real
It startles me to tears.
He's gone, back to whatever world
We only know in dreams or wistfulness.
But his presence shook my daytime daze
And left behind some childhood truth,
A high, sweet never-ending note
To listen for, and follow
Through the maze.

At The Turning of the Glass

I

That was half my life ago,
I know;
But did I, was I, will I
Know
When it is, was, will be
Half my life ago
Again?

II

Somehow I chose to put aside the palette
To pick up the charcoal and the pen.
Perhaps the parallel
To drying joints and muscles
Is a preference for the pallid,
A sort of sunglass for the soul.

III

Some turn to stronger foods
Because the tastebuds
No longer are in flower;
Others find the stomach shrinks
Away from what the mind
Appears to crave.
Disproportion is the enzyme
That processes the world.

IV

A kind of compensation emerges
As a whimsy,
A puckering of purpose,
A beautiful indifference
That is suspended
At real difference.
And while imbalance sways the scales
The balancing goes on.

City Courtyard

Fifty years ago a tiny boy, whose life
I seem to recollect, peered through
A shabby kitchen window
Into the yard below.
It was a sort of no-man's land
Between four tenements, crisscrossed
By clotheslines hung like banners
Overhead. Sometimes in spring
Lazy dust-mote spirals rose gently
Through the sunny air, and sounds
Of muffled voices floated,
With rich smells of Sunday breakfasts,
From a hidden world across the yard.
In winter, at times a ragged violinist
Played standing in the snow,
For coins tossed down from windows
By disembodied hands.
There was a little roof, atop a little building,
Just below a window, that I loved.
It was flat and square, a little
Lower than my window perch,
Asphalt-black, with vivid plants
In reds and greens along the edge.
It was a stage for my imagination,
But the plays I made are now
Forever gone, unless some other child
Preserves them in some secret way.
One day a lady leaned out
Upon the roof, and waved,
And then my mother handed me
The red toy car the lady sent.
I liked the car, and wondered
Why the lady sent it.
But soon I stopped such thoughts,
And turned away from dreaming
At the window, and closed my days
Of looking at the yard.

Echoes: 1949

I have made a study of self...
...and found I was a stranger...
I have sat in the darkened room
of my mind
and watched the pale glimmer of my
flickering thought
tracing strange patterns on the wall
like the errant beams
of light
from the passing autos gleaming fitfully
on the shadowed pulsing living walls
and fading...gently...
while the sickness in my stomach
makes the silence hum a silent dirge
for the dusty pictures hanging
on the shadowed walls
while the creeping coldness in my spine
sets the colors
whirling blue-purple through the cloying air
shrieking in its silence
from the aching bittersweet longing
for something
I cannot name...
and the plaintive notes of a concert piano
mingling strangely
with the burning echoing glory of
the midnight sky
        ...for Auld Lang Syne...
and the creeping warmth of the knowledge of a
million
sensations impulses animosities desires
        ...for Auld Lang Syne...
...fading gently...
        ...for Auld Lang Syne...
...fading gently...
        ...for Auld Lang Syne...
...fading...gently...
I have made a study of self...
...and found I was a stranger...

Beyond the Maze

So finally the maze no longer mocks.
Within my gaze the hedges straighten out;
The path disdains another cruel divide.
Somewhat like that ancient prince
Who ran the Cretan labyrinth,
For me, no monsters linger
In my past, my strength
Must grow from having won
Where others failed.
But Theseus had adventures, glories
Yet to come. For me the challenge
Lies behind a simple garden gate
Which I approach at lovely end of day.
There is no way to go except
The path; my task will be
To listen to the counsel of the birds,
To taste the rain and grass
That vinify the air, and read
The semaphore of trees
While still there is some light.

Galileo

Radio telescopes and human prayers
Agitate the cosmos
Searching
For God's ears.

Epitaph

Poems are like snowflakes
Intricate and fragile
Shimmering for an instant
In the wintry air
Vanishing forever
When they touch
The barren ground.